SKY. POND. MOUTH.

KEVIN MCLELLAN

"Kevin McLellan's *Sky. Pond. Mouth.* is my new favorite book of poems. I could read it every day forever for its tender curiosity about the geranium on the table and the two men dressed alike in the laundromat, and its patient pacing through the quietly threatening world. Every line and metaphor is adventurous and thorough in documenting the longing and doubt invested in every moving and every still thing. *The earth is dying but we don't notice it,* someone says in the poem "Blue," but this book notices, and it notices the housefly, and the crumpled paper, and the desire and distance between men—all clearly visible through and against McLellan's quiet wisdom."

— Lisa Lewis is the author of *Silent Treatment*, winner of the National Poetry Series, and several other books.

Yas Press
University of New Hampshire
English Department
230 Hamilton Smith Hall
Durham, NH 03824
All rights reserved, including right of
reproduction in whole or part in any form.

Cover art © Kevin McLellan
Text © 2024 by Kevin McLellan

Cover and interior designer: Ashley Halsey
Managing editor: Molly McGrath
Published in partnership with Pink Eraser Press

CONTENTS

Introduction   7

ECOSYSTEMS
Ecosystem   *13*
Clouds   *15*
A Definition of Loss   *17*
Always Something Falling   *19*
Sheep Laurel   *21*
Swamp Rose   *23*
Bloodroot   *25*
Interrupted Fern   *27*
Floriculture   *29*
The Geranium   *31*
Glimmer   *33*
The Estate   *35*
Narrative   *37*

THE CORRIDOR
The Corridor   *47*

OTHER INDICES; AND THE EAVES

Regarding What Was Lost Before I Knew It Was Taken   *57*
Blue   *65*
Too Bright for Landscapes   *67*
Ashbery   *69*
A Housefly   *71*
The Blue Vehicle   *73*
It Fell   *75*
The Crumpled Paper   *77*
Iron   *79*
James Schuyler to John Ashbery   *81*
Dear James Schuyler,   *83*
Comeuppance   *85*
Viridescent Varieties   *87*
Colored Condoms   *91*
Limbs   *93*
On Variation   *95*
Pinyon   *97*
On the Other Side   *99*
A Myth   *111*

WINTERBERRIES

Winterberries   *115*

Afterword   *133*
Acknowledgments   *134*

INTRODUCTION

Sky. Pond. Mouth. is a book that doesn't take much for granted—boundaries, solidity, distinctions between plants and humans, lasting companionship, faith, enduring self, health. This is a poetry of ontology, permeable and mutually dependent. Every noun is potentially non-I *and* I. The isolated being is the connected being and vice-versa in a constant turn-over of needing & peace-of-mind, needing & peace-of-mind.

Starting with the book's title, physical and emotional qualities range freely between the animate and inanimate as though the world is written with dotted lines. "Freedom," McLellan quotes A.R. Ammons, might be "identity without identity," an untethering even from untethering. In the long poem "Winterberries," as an example, "The wind made the light and an ash / tree seem one, animated yet mortal, / and then it ceased. For a moment / I thought the statue in the park / was me, not *of me*. (Sometimes one / needs to tell someone to go away.)" The sensual and the corporeal are geographic.

Somehow, what McLellan posits is utterly realistic. More so than a surreal Scotch-taping of an object onto an unexpected location, a sewing machine and an umbrella's encounter on an operating table. On every page, I was shown a new way of understanding being alive. McLellan's poetic position recalls Marcus Aurelius in *Meditations*: "The world as a living being—one nature, one soul. Keep that in mind. And how everything feeds into that single experience, moves with a single motion." Or (also Aurelius): "Yesterday a blob of semen; tomorrow embalming fluid, ash."

It's not always comfortable. It's frankly a bit lonesome. In *Sky. Pond. Mouth.*, a person might well be "benthic," or located at the bottom of a large water body. The climate setting is dialed to thawing solitude and to the temperature on the ocean floor. In "Clouds," a pond "stretches out" in the speaker's chest as the consequence of the loss of love, that is, of being in love for five minutes. In the forest setting of the prose poem "A Definition of Loss," trees are equipped with "mouth holes too," forming an orchestra which the poet joins as a soloist. Although this tree-and-human ensemble wouldn't be possible without his bravely different perceptions, the speaker's not certain that his fellow performers actually hear him.

A theme of *Sky. Pond. Mouth.* is patience: it's worth it. The drifting away from set forms is necessary for knowing more, knowing better, knowing how to know. Staying unbroken or holding the expected form only blocks our perceptions because, as McLellan says, DNA strands and a pair of eyes "know things despite their connectedness."

Literal human interactions in *Sky. Pond. Mouth.* reinforce the book's metaphysics. Solo passengers on cell phones are overheard on a long bus ride to Berlin, New Hampshire, and men observed trying to hook up. This poet is a people watcher: an observer of our back-and-forth dotted line existence of connection with others and connection with self. Writing teachers fall silent in the classroom at a gap even in poetry's gap-loving expressiveness. Older parents are too chatty too early in the morning at the kitchen table.

In the Ecosystems section early in this book, there's a series of persona poems in which the speaker crosses over to a plant (swamp rose, bloodroot, sheep laurel), a member of a marshland or renter of the unmown, not so much a flowerbed or community garden club. These plants contemplate celibacy or reject labels and judgment. Resembling illustrations of single specimens from a botanical book, they're like the poems in the book as a whole: distinct. McLellan doesn't repeat himself in this collection of prose poetry to lyric poems to longer sectioned exposition. With chiseled line breaks, intriguing meta-poetic levels, and punctuation like seed pods, these poems, if we look twice, might flourish outside the book's margin, past the grow light of the screen, even (especially) other borderlines we haven't begun to imagine.

Alexandria Peary
New Hampshire Poet Laureate
Judge of the 2024 Granite State Poetry Prize
January 5, 2024

ECOSYSTEMS

ECOSYSTEM

Here, a valley. Here, the likelihood of wind—a catalogue of matter, the findings not unlike double negatives. I look for answers from the wellspring. Find this collision of monosyllables—*the sky on top of the pond*. These words must mean something. In a mirror my face becomes a run-on sentence, and the syntax of eyes requires translation. These parallel mirrors take in and emit, transmit a series of unique frequencies. Each slightly different from the previous like a series of movie frames or DNA strands. They know things despite their connectedness. My body's ear detects their signals. Yet the lack of awareness is mine. Imagine: a ripe carrot propelling itself out of the ground or a snail leaving its cornucopian dome. Imagine: the *I don't want to die* motivation we wake-up to each morning. Imagine: a sky on top of a pond in a valley. Here, low clouds—like winter lily pads—hang with their half-submerged thoughts.

CLOUDS

The rope whips against
the flag pole. I miss hearing
him say *we*, yet I wasn't
the one. Yes, he was thinking

about someone else and
I look to the sky. Painters
need to know the sky—always
a witness. And birds too,

realists, yet we often don't
pay them any attention.
Did you hear me? I was
in love for five minutes.

And then the pond
stretched out inside my chest.

A DEFINITION OF LOSS

The mouth of the cave is hungry which is why a bear with a mouth hole lives here. All the moss outside the cave. All the trees. All the trees here have mouth holes too. The trees' holes, an orchestra, and I, a soloist, so a concerto. Though I am not sure if I am heard. Inversely, the wind, an invisible bow, forces tree language. There's a bottle here on the forest floor. The winds and the bottle create a concerto which is heard. The mouth of the canyon yawns again, but not out of boredom—another kind of music. The mouth of the sky. The mouth of the sky is vast and everything around it evasive, especially clouds.

ALWAYS SOMETHING FALLING

in the forest. Surrounded
by rooted earth, only lines
& shapes prime for bears.
Maybe spirits? The lake

is a mirror, then it isn't. Only
the memory of it. Yesterday
the moisture on the bottom
of my tent I realize today

might be condensation from
my own breath that beaded
above my head & the-once-
a-part-of-me rained. Now, in

front of an early morning
campfire, I squint. *Field Notes
on a Moth.* The last time I saw
one it was grounded by heavy

rain in front of the recently
fallen, not felled, widow-maker.
It kept trying. It kept trying
& the grass so green around it.

SHEEP LAUREL

a thing for shade
& peat bogs i
also kill pigs

& lambs &
calves & after
the fire & after

the loggers
evergreen
narrow-leaved

me—took over;
seeds turned
180 degrees

for the early
bees & my crimson-
pink—sure—

go ahead—tease me.

SWAMP ROSE

damned
at the out-
set: name

akin to a girl
who town
-to-towned

or an ab-
staining
queer

who once
slept
around—i

am both
naïve & away
running

though not
seizing
a swamp

—nor
a swamp
over me.

BLOODROOT

'cause of all the O's

'cause rooted in taint
'cause no nectar

'cause red—'cause

white petals but it's
the stamen's yellow

that makes me feel

dirty—& i is we &
we're queer-

ing underground like

Gen Xers closing it
all down or the celibate

at nightfall for yet

another summer 'cause
suicidal petals 'cause

yellow 'cause

exposure 'cause
all of it back in the day;

INTERRUPTED FERN

gap—blade—gap

—my portions died
back—the blade—

back into the gap—

bipinnate blade—gap
—but turn it on baby

—turn it on—drop

the furl—one frond
—two—Triassic.

FLORICULTURE

We are all already dead.

The flower box doesn't care.

The seated man frequently raises one sinewy arm above his head.

Only the skin between the bottom of the tee and the top of jeans shows.

When he stands to leave the slack in the fold fills.

I want the petunias to care.

THE GERANIUM

I look out the window, wait
for you, envy all
the outdoors' moving
parts. The geranium

on the kitchen table, red
next to the window, also
waits. This blooming privy
to my secrets. Its language

isn't translatable; scent,
a gesture. The last time
you were here you said,
I am like a fish. I can go

anywhere, and I knew that
this was a warning.

GLIMMER

the window left open—pollen
—finger—evidence of
being there—don't care if
allergic—touch my other
hand—imagine him—
ask "what's inside the inside"—
thalamus insists on *let me*—
no difference between
orgasm & orange blossom
& sneeze—instead focus
now on the bedroom floor
open to the outside
light—light also burnishing
these white open doors—

THE ESTATE

Night wanders
permanently
and I can only think about
sliced apples.

Or willingness.
The meat separated
from the skin
and I squeeze my lip

in lieu of seeing this hay
being put down.
Forlorn I was told
and *too soon*.

By night we're separated—
so I will one day.

NARRATIVE

~~The lawn. Then~~ the unkempt
brush. ~~Yesterday~~ an innocuous

snake ~~in front of me. & on both
sides, like margins, tree-lines~~

~~& of course the leaning
trees. In mid-ground,~~ canting

cows ~~once grazed.~~ The hay
overgrown. ~~The last time~~

~~I visited a bear & her cubs
crossed the field. & deer too.~~

~~A hill~~ & behind that hill
~~a mountain. But here the house~~

~~sits on the side of another
mountain.~~ Imagine: ~~all of this~~

~~slanted,~~ the sideways ~~5 o'clock
light,~~ dome-pitching ~~shadows~~

~~across just peaked, just detached
leaves,~~ & an early owl sounding.

I had

the concept of before and after. I walk
toward the boy on fire.
I tell myself. Shh…, and then
a flicker:
sitting on a last stair looking

looking back. Learned—
from men who know how to gut
fish—that the proliferating
moth will proliferate
in the walnuts.

someone else's dreams. He
didn't know

Shh…,

it's me!

a camera
in the face, but I can't see who is

Say, *cheese*!

The sign on the library lawn: *ground*
                                 under
                                 repair
and my favorite wordsmith, who I believe
would appreciate this succession
of words, died on my birthday, the man
who I had admired from afar
earlier that day was leaning against
the Elm St. house in Cambridge
on a Friday night
        rubbed ~~his~~
        crotch ~~as he~~
        smiled ~~at me~~
or during the same week in Stillwater,
just after the stallion-red midterm elections,
the handsome man waiting for a to-go coffee
bashfully
        looked ~~over and~~
        smiled ~~at me and then~~
        walked
through the kitchen doors—the same
by association these elusive men,
including the wordsmith, and I can't stop
                      indexing.

Thinking about what Ed said in LOST HIGHWAY, *I like to remember things my own way... how I remembered them. Not necessarily the way they happened;* sitting in the first row of the balcony, like at Club Silencio where Betty and Camilla (or was she Rita then?) sat crying in MULHOLLAND DRIVE, until overcome with vertigo I fell head first into the unoccupied row of seats below.

I died at the end of the Lynch double feature.

—

I find myself wearing white shirts and traveling by train more often, a place between places. The docks and harbor are quiet today. No metal on metal. No fish heads. But now the blur of green from trees and the rise and dip of power lines like waves until this stretch of real estate is behind buildings, a burial ground for things; what have I forgotten?

—

Storiesaboutstraightxxxhavinggaysex.
Manhumpsamericanflagpillowtoorgasm.
Regularlookingguysnakedsex.

Powertopforbottom.
Uncutdocking.
Suckingahotuberdriver.

—

"Why?" PrEP and some awareness means that the rates are down. "Why?" It seems only the current definitions of *queer* and *gay* are relevant to my contemporaries. It has always been about currency.

—

The recycling men left scraps of paper on the sidewalk like body parts, torn-up earlier drafts of this poem;	my earliest memory involves a staircase and a marble, not people.

—

A man I don't know is biking and I recognize his suffering. He pedals evenly, leans forward not unlike a rower, and his thick hair has taken the shape from this ride.

—

A yellow jacket in my face, so from the shade into the sun I move;	the sliver of shadows seems permanent outside.

OR

Inside, the sun motes I try to grip;	I am separated from direct sunlight despite being pressed up against the window.

—

I become separated. We could see one another until the deluge. They had shelter. I didn't. I shout, "When will I next see you?" They respond, *may the sea be calm for you.*

—

30 years earlier: your apartment above Bagdad Café on Market Street. The neon red glare and the glare of my early mouth. You asserted too much for me. Desire, also too much then. We tried until, *never mind*—your grace with offhandedness and my flickering neon. We wouldn't meet again, yet the naked image of you watching me leave succeeds.

I have no other family, though there are many, and look to the world [stanza break] for stability. But it is accelerating more. & yes I am hypercritical. For example: I walked home after the documentary about water, walked fast because it was raining. Didn't I learn [stanza break] anything? The rain stirred up the rag- & milk- weed, & my acceleration. But now I am sitting in an Adirondack blowing my nose. The crows here [stanza break] caw in threes. A cricket lost its long-jump. The ferns will return [stanza break] when they feel like it. The time of day when all the nearby animals hide behind trees. The trees detached from those about to [stanza break] detach. The wind accelerates. The leaves too. It just happens. Not for some humans. For example: I resist [stanza break] the narrative. See it as insignificant. & especially when insistent. Though resist them less when I am in nature. & I am in nature.

THE CORRIDOR

THE CORRIDOR

As a child a painted turtle found me, so I made a cage for him, but by the next morning he had disappeared. I assumed that the turtle was a him because I was a him and needed to be found.

—

Ammons was onto something when he asked, *is freedom identity without identity?*

—

I cannot not look at the back of the man's shaved head. His occipital lobe and neck twitch. A neurological trauma? When he boarded the bus I detected confidence and defeat. A grave demeanor. His handsomeness. It appeared to me that he needed care, and I imagined him with me.

—

I want to know what monks do at night, how they handle their bodies and surprise.

—

It is as if desire takes a snapshot of the man that prompted said desire and these snapshots collectively influence the itch growing within the groin's groin.

—

I notice two young men. One's much taller than the other. The shorter one's asleep, head resting on the tall one's shoulder. They don't speak English. This is what brotherhood looks like in many countries, but not America. There is another man in his twenties on this bus, but he sits alone. I heard him say to another passenger that he's going to Berlin. The other Berlin. The one in New Hampshire. He has many tattoos on his hands. He wears a gray hoodie, a black baseball cap with a round decal on the visor, Malcolm X eyeglasses, and bright red sneakers. He listens to EDM, and during a phone *convo* tells his friend to *stop buggin' out*.

—

From this great distance the dark clouds behind the white ones look like a large mountain. We talk about getting ice cream, but my father stays home. He doesn't like to venture. I feel guilty.

—

Have I become too personal here?

—

My mother says, *they changed the weather* and I correct her each time. Why this impulse to revise her? I know she meant to say, *they changed the forecast*. She wakes from her own talking. This is what I tell her. When she talks in the morning I tell her that I need mornings to be quiet. But this morning, for this first time, she said nothing, and it felt like death. There is a mother who likes to talk and nearby birds flutter to all the windows to hear her. No. There is a mother who likes to talk to her son in the morning and he likes to hear her talk. No.

———

I break each morning as if emerging from the sea—this underworld of disorientation and gasp, and the pressing thoughts about entering a room.

———

My friend's six-year-old screams for an hour this morning before church because he can't find any clothes that feel good. Another child tells me in a dream, *just because I am a conduit doesn't mean that I am a parrot!*

———

I understand that this vocabulary is overused: *heart, silence,* and *nothingness* (Ammons' favorite word). I refer to birds too often.

—

I notice how much more feeble my dad has become. He says, *it will expire on July 31st,* but he's talking about a buy-one-get-one-free coupon for pizza. The English language confuses me. How *is* your dad? and How *are* you? I don't know how to answer.

—

nothingness

—

Two men walk into a Laundromat. They wear identical neon jackets with thin black stripes. Earlier, the taller one asked if there were bathrooms here. The other asked how long I'd been here and if I'd seen a Swisher Sweets tin. They just returned and the shorter one asks if there is a bathroom here and I say, *you asked this before.* He responds, *that wasn't me that asked— it was him.*

—

In New Hampshire, driving with a friend late at night, our headlights suddenly shine on the explicit inside-out pink of a deer, its meat, and then an 18-wheeler on the side of the road.

—

Or the dog owner reads a newspaper. I feel tense passing his bull terrier on a leash. After I pass, the sudden sound of two dogs, one lunges at another. I feel responsible.

—

Or I take my time this morning and while waiting for the bus hear a woman on her cell ask, *why call me if you're not going to talk?*

—

Or I was running late, as were the buses. I didn't know this until it was too late.

—

This wind will make the mind fall down and dearest word, any word, please leave the indoors for outside. As I get older robins allow me to get closer.

—

I write the following in a letter, "Carpe diem. Denim. Carpet. Rug. Ragout. Dug out. Out of the closet. There are reasons to hide."

OTHER INDICES; AND THE EAVES

REGARDING WHAT WAS LOST BEFORE I KNEW IT WAS TAKEN

> *To exist in public demands performance*
> -Tony Kushner

8:00 a.m. on Memorial Day and from inside a café I wave to the pacing man outside who I misrecognized. He takes his pulse in front of this huge open window. The sky is calm, a scattering of clouds. I imagine them wanting to hold more. Two birds fuck-fly around, a-round into the street, almost get struck by a moving car.

[
from my window
the limp body
I saw carried
from my window
facing theirs
the man inside
being carried
by his lover
from my window
]

But again, in front of this window. A man in black shorts and a tight t-shirt locks his bike in the just-available spot. His movements are precise. He and the bike are relaxed, poised. Me? Uptight in loose sweatpants and a sweatshirt. My bike? Upright and locked to a parking meter. Opposites? Opposites! But I have learned passivity from, and since, the origins of shouting, so I don't know the ground rules for communicating with a contemporary. Am I self-mythologizing again?

> [
> naïve
> with spikes
> like loosestrife. I took
> too much
> time. Conflict? No
> true lines
> to the body
> when no one
> touches them.
>]

Is it the man I noticed at the laundromat?

    I recognized him by the way his ass lifts his skinny jeans and how quickly he devours a Camel Light. As a younger man I was objectified on a regular basis. Learned behavior?

Is it the manager at the natural foods market?

    He relocated product with a co-worker. Our eyes locked. I went back the next day to give him my number. He didn't acknowledge me. As if the look we shared never happened.

Is it the inked man?

    Not the one with the southern accent going on and on about himself and scorpions, but rather the quiet one with piercings who looked at me with intent and curiosity?

Is it the quiet man entering the pharmacy as I left?

    I recognized him from the restaurant down the street. He has a large mouth. I unlocked my bike, leaned it against the bench just outside, and waited for him to leave. He seems to own only one pair of jeans. They're oversized. He's short. He passed me and glanced back.

> [
> the day before
> the night
> I took *the cocktail*:
> the parking lot:
> a dumpster:
> the courthouse
> down the hill:
> the overpass: I
> am standing
> inside my stomach
> breathing
> unevenly
> facing a train station
>]

Is it the man who changed his gait to let his penis move more freely?

    Any man who changes his gait for this reason? So this is just about sex then?

Is it the man who turned down a blind date, said he'd call and didn't?

    So instead I friended him on Facebook—he accepted, yet no follow up thus far from either of us.

Is it the man with a wild look in his eyes who stood on the corner near my apartment?

Out the window I looked	; looking up he saw me looking down.
Downstairs	; he stood facing the street with his back to my front door, followed as I walked toward a side street.
It started sprinkling and I looked back;	he leaned against a house and rubbed his crotch.
His eyes shifted	; I walked toward the park, turned, and discovered he hadn't followed me.
The rain fell harder	; he ran toward Main Street.

                              [
                the time I let a man
                      at a bar take
                      me to a lake
                  house (remember
          only a surface) (a dark
                    mirror) outside
                      the city limits
                    and leading up
                   to sex I wanted
                    to leave but
            asking him for a ride
                    seemed more
                              unsafe
                                   ]

Is it the focused man at the cafe who sat at the same table with me?

My arms pressed firmly against the long narrow plank; when he struck the laptop keys the table shifted, rocked my body. I felt close to him.

                              [
              the too-numerous
                              times
                      my father's
                        pounding
                            hands
        behind my running feet

on the staircase
and the other pounding
in my throat
before I became
invisible
to him
]

Is it the man who camped beside me with his five boys and a wife?

    I didn't clearly hear his voice until the third day. He facilitated a made-up geography game for his sons the day of the thunderstorm when he escorted each of them, one-by-one, to the showers. They rode their bikes, but the last one said he didn't want to bike in the rain. The father said, *do you want to walk then?* When the father walked by he looked for me; when I looked in his direction he looked away. I did the same. Is this homophobia?

Is it the man who walked toward me in the rain?

    He carefully lifted his umbrella above mine. I felt close to him.

[
the moment I
no longer
needed
to fear
the given
you-are-positive

>   news/taken
>   within
>   ]

Again, in front of the giant window, but this time on the outside looking in. I see a blurred man holding: a book, his composure, a contemplative expression, and an empty demitasse; I am: the refracted light, the book, a blurred man, and just an ordinary man.

BLUE
(after the Derek Jarman film)

When I look into, not at, the screen—
the blinking red and green

pixels frantic behind blue, but I
can't walk too long behind this sky—

notice the exit sign and the left side
of flickering faces. I must return

to where you sit, once sat,
behind blue. The textured collage

of sounds a way to make sense
of, what you call, 'abnormal thoughts'

and I feel a heartbeat in the eyes—
a throbbing experience

onto the screen. I must shut them
again. A second hand and the hour

bells sound simultaneously, continue
as you say, *the earth is dying and we don't
notice it.* Then the sound of rain.
You mention delphiniums once more.

TOO BRIGHT FOR LANDSCAPES

The legends egress, left us

unattended. How much of
the world doesn't want me?

Who, without toying, will

hold my head in his lap?
This position of intimate

implications, but my mouth

doesn't concern you. I'm not
a jack-in-the-box or a feather

in your cap. Somewhere

an assault is happening.
I am not unlike you, a holding

cell for ancestral passages

and glyphs. They're sequestered
in marrow and in the mind.

I trust that mine wouldn't

approve because I am also
in the lap of a meadow

with my mouth wide open.

ASHBERY

I missed your last reading
in order to *approximate*

real time for the audience. You

know, I needed to think
more about the *you*'s,

my *you*'s. Nothing lovelier

than paper, right? If only
I had had wheels, though

imagine a wary mountain

queer worrying in Princeton!
Going awry's why I have

known division intimately.

Poetry separates further. Shall I
return to the valley of Canada

geese & black sheep, Ashbery?

I would have asked you if
you wore Gore-Tex

and what happens when

one doesn't cross the aisle
anymore? I must entertain

the notion of forward.

A HOUSEFLY

The housefly
on the glass. The housefly
on the glass
cover. The glass cover
on the pie plate
holding part of
a pie. I stare at
      what remains
      of the pie
        the exposed insides
        made from
        the insides
        of apples. The fly
on the glass cover
flies away
and I feel lost

      again. I feel lost
      and I am looking
      at glass

      then around the room.
The room is small.
The room knows. The room
knows me better

than most. My eyes.
I am looking *through*
the glass. Not at a fly
      nor at glass
      or pie or part of
one. At a tree. A tree
      trunk. I am looking
      at a tree trunk.
      Sunlight. The wind.
      Sunlight
      and the shadows
      on itself.

      The leaves on itself.

THE BLUE VEHICLE

I am looking at the blue vehicle
parked out front. I am blue.
      But I am parked inside
during work hours. Parked
inside during daylight. I am not shiny
nor electric blue
like the vehicle parked out front.
      Who sees me
when I am out front? I am between
navy and midnight. Somewhere
between navy and midnight
the week before Daylight Savings
      Time. We are different
models. Different years.
I wheel the streets
with all the others going
at different speeds. Different
      places. We are going
to different places. Different
shades. I am as visible as
midnight blue. I am midnight
blue and it is dusk. I am not
      noticeable. I am midnight
      and I am out front.

IT FELL

The white car draws near white out.
Parallel trees on the side of the road.

My perpendicular eyes.
Perpendicular memory.

I imagine backyard trees.
What are backyard trees to do?

Elsewhere a sidewalk.
Parallel sidewalks.

Even more lines in conflict.
And my memory of lines.

The sidewalk. The house across the street.
Accidental bikes forced upright.

My perpendicular memory.
A brick house across the street.

Parallel bricks. Their building.
Their conflicted lines.

Snow on the screen. Almost outside.
The house across the street.

And my memory.
My memory of weighted tree limbs.

Freezing point and the street below.
The lines. Ice.

Roof. Snow. Plane.
Ice under the eaves.

The plane's sound. Snow.
What the snow became.

A yellow tulip.
What are flowers to do?

Freezing point and the street below.
A car after the white.

A van between two lines.
White vehicles.

THE CRUMPLED PAPER

In the subway station
at the bottom of
the stairwell
the crumpled piece

      of paper. The conflicting
      air currents. The different
      trains. Quick. The rolling
      & skidding. The straightening wall

& bottom stair
riser. Quick & jagged
90 degree arcs. I can't
escape it. The crumpled paper.

      Record the conflicting
      air currents
      on video. On my phone.
      I had traveled from the bus

station. & before that
the ride itself. On a bus
from the straightening
little town I left.

IRON

The 4:00. Provincetown-to-Boston

carries less than 20 of us. No one

else here, stern & starboard: the

2nd floor. I think, *dignity directly*

corresponds to a face—my face &

persona just dismissed by a fellow

fellow—& I fixate on the rolling

whitecaps. The fog lifting & the

lighthouse no longer in view. No

boats either. No birds. No other

passengers. I hear myself sternly

say to myself, "It's deep" & now

a sinking feeling, the vertical pull

from stomach to toes—all soles.

JAMES SCHUYLER TO JOHN ASHBERY
(in memory of Karl Tierney)

We are tentative.
We are tentatively looking.
Landscapes unknown.
We are tentatively looking for landscapes unknown to us.
Our window.
Our window is a square.
Our window is a beautiful unlatched square picture window
  and we are tentatively looking.
Our window is ours, not the powers' that be
  and is beautiful and unlatched
  and we are beautiful and not unlatched
  and we are tentatively looking
  and do not feel a bit disturbed or troubled.
We have the light on
  and then do not.
First we have the light on, for the people
  and then we have it off, for ourselves.
No, ourselves is a lie
  for there is always darkness.
We have the direction of darkness
  so ourselves is a lie
  when we have the light on.
In the darkness is your yellow cardigan
  and our window is a square.

A square. Yes, a square
        and your yellow cardigan is in the darkness
        from your beautiful unlatched square picture window.
Your yellow cardigan is shrouding
        for we are tentatively looking
        towards landscapes that do not
        give us any indication of the other.
Tentatively, yes, tentatively looking we are
        in a beautiful square picture window
        but neither unlatched nor green
        nor very distracted or troubled, really.
We are merely tentative
        and can be seen with the light on
        in the direction of darkness.

DEAR JAMES SCHUYLER,

Cut coral-red-colored roses   & I
     (with your book) reflected
in the glass:
     the outside glass door
overlooking the dark
street; now, thunder & lightning
creates shadows:
     Japanese Red Maple branches
& freeze-framed
     raindrops (and their shadows)
appear solid
for a split second;   a soaked moth
not in my face
     my twitching hand
swats & I don't recognize my ghost
hand   (turning your page);   now;

COMEUPPANCE

sold my boots soon after
      the Pistyll
Rhaeadr waterfalls & then
      the 20-
         year pout
after our break & like loose-
      strife
         on the edges
of a rock garden i had just laid
      there—laid
      there!
deracinated—now a beginning
      -to-lose-balance
expression on the apple-face
      selling
         reduced peppers—
when i get home halve them—
      two sets
         of green ears
before me—remember his
      enlarged ones—
      remember
      standing &
      waving goodbye
to him on a hill where we'll

           never return—
around the time of learned
           violation—
the feeling of cars driving over
           my shadow—
edges smoothing out & then
           disappeared
like him & while overthinking
           things i missed

the lunar eclipse—treetops.

VIRIDESCENT VARIETIES

i   *Manifold*

a benthic man
returns
to his home-
town & folds
& all of

my onesome
holds an empty
potato chip bag

ii *Still Life with Geranium*

the great head
of winter &
a stunted plant
of two minds
in the window—
& the sound of
an owl—a man
sounding
downstairs—
arouses
occasion

& occlusion—I
am all &
already ready

iii.   *Passe-partout*

three streets—
the triangular island
with two trees—
all the arresting
mature
velvet
violet
tulips'
mouths

wide open

& I am too
late for
prospicience

iv   *The Bosky Edge*

a headlamp
on night-water
looks like
a boot print
with medical
imaging
rippling
over—
sthenic—
skirring—
reifying

the oddments—go
toward
the sward—yes

COLORED CONDOMS
(after Gertrude Stein)

Colored condoms are necessary. They reflect the variety of ways to protect oneself and others from routine and this makes a difference for outies and innies, inclusive terminology for all the bottoms out there. Out there, something else tightens and broad stomachs await the big delay. So lovely the light when it shows a swatch of upstaging skin, and all the custard shades.

LIMBS
(after Gertrude Stein)

A sough, a sough
not different from
ours, a sough in
sequence. Suppose
there is a lone
pinyon & lone
flume. Just suppose
there is, okay?
        Loneliness,
a mirror in the

bedroom, there is
a mirror in the
bedroom & what
doesn't appear
to be the same?
An era of things
doesn't appear the
same when a mirror's
in the bedroom.

The era when there
were options. When

there are options. This
        is specificity.
        Spe-ci-fi-city.
Suppose there's a
limb. Suppose there
are limbs. There are
limbs. When there are
limbs there's to be

        activity?
        Inactivity?
There are limbs &
there is desire. A
fixed way to think
about difference
is to imagine.
Imagine showing
likeness, okay?

ON VARIATION

Sometimes the words left
the intended order.
The intended order left
the words sometimes.

Left the words sometimes
the intended order. The words
left the intended order
sometimes. Order sometimes

the words left the intended.
The intended order sometimes
the words left. The words
order sometimes left the

intended. Sometimes the
intended order the words left.

PINYON

Pinyon. Chimney

      smoke. High
      altitude.

      The burning. I had

      stayed
one night in a small bed

with a small man in a small

      hotel burning
      pinyon. Hotel.

      Man. Bed

That I slipped out of. Away
from. Pinyon. Sweet

as innocence. The smoke

wafting. Out of. Away
from. The chimney. Pinyon

      at high altitudes.

ON THE OTHER SIDE

i.   A FAIRY TALE

Once there was a man.

He kept his basketball
underneath the pinball

machine he was playing

in an underground bar.
The center of my body

called out to his. And

his response was to let
silver roll down the center.

ii.   INTERCOURSE

The details

of urge
mislead

and I forget

to ask,
"Where am I

now?" Now

the familiar
walk back

to start over,

take inventory—
colors. I am

made of colors.

iii.   ASUNDER

Strangers look

blankly through
me. Now another

on the other side

of a plate-glass
window. I'm not

religious, learned

this when I locked
eyes with cast iron,

a gate which usurped

a willingness to
introduce myself. I

can no longer assume

that person, a break
in the mirror, when

in parallel. Eyes are

uncertain. "How did I
get here"? My body,

a new form, rejects

in sunder, skin and
language await

this bright morning.

iv.   BOYFRIEND

Of another

horizon, now
upright,

in the in-

between
two

worlds,

though your
musculature

can adapt

only for so
long, the

length of it

uncertain
no matter

the orientation.

v.   SYSTEMS

Yet another thinning voice has something to say.

One experiences memory in twilight in a field differently.

Okay, the voice is mine.

Nature insists on coupling.

We are each a soundtrack for loss.

But it's too late for home-schooling.

vi.   *PLAID*

For so long I will

reach past my skin
toward others, envy

the singularity

of both the red
and the black in

this stranger's shirt—

vii.   *THE MEN INSIDE*

A storm rustling the trees,

circulating snow—I am
so obvious, don't know how

to be delicate or subtle. Plows,

also men, push my essence
out of the way. Other men find

a wind too much for them or

a window screen collecting
windblown snow.

I am also the man inside.

viii.   AERIAL VIEW: AFTER A HOMOSEXUAL ACT

The evening, a place to enter

with grace, and the table
a perfect place to consummate.

Just because it isn't happening

to you doesn't mean it isn't
happening. The cinder block

wall might judge, yet the ceiling

understands the nature of above.
And below. The knocked over

vase once on the table rests

on its side. In its trail of drink.
On the cool tiles beside the tulips.

ix.   TWINE

The body stores fat, pain,
memories, and shame.

This morning the two red tulips

beheaded in a loft. Their heads
on the white tile belong to their

stems. I can't relate to pairs, so

what color am I? A bouquet
taken out of the water, its legs

tied with twine and hung upside

down. After my first experience,
I cried too.

x.   *WHEN THE PATIO BECOMES THE ATTIC*

The chest, long emptied
of its heirlooms, understands

stones. The stones continue

missing the field. I relate
to field, stones and chest, yet

can't reconcile or remember

the first time I recognized
myself in a mirror, everything

and nothing. Or perhaps I've

mistaken myself for plastic
lawn furniture. Or a rake.

A MYTH

Either way, they will need to organize the road closing over the next few rainy nights. To determine if this water is a small pond or a vernal pool, a scientist collects evidence. After disturbances, and there are plenty, their heartbeats slow. This species can be found across the forehead of open woods near water, solitary along forest edges, or on the underside of fruit (cashews, dates, and figs). They are attracted to golden tints and for this reason alone they're vulnerable. Other than the position of the head, there are no distinct characteristics. In some lifestyles, like theirs, the rump gives signals. In opposition to popular opinion, their openings must not be blocked.

WINTERBERRIES

WINTERBERRIES

i.

My thoughts have no place
to go, except more inward—
I focus on the frozen river,
those I don't allow to reach
me. The boat is a liar and I
will not listen. Kites are also
liars. Never mind—I know
who I am: male, female, and
neither. I judge indecision
and refusal. *Long live the
queen* also means the king
is dead. In other words,
I'm a eunuch and I'm looking
to the river. Dare I say
the viaduct is arrhythmic?
I'd tell the engineers, but they
are too busy talking among
themselves. Somewhere, there's
an ocean, a wellspring and in
the in-between, a pulse. I talk
to myself. So a thinness of skin.
A galaxy with dangling lights,
each bulb in a glass enclosure,

yet assembled together and
hanging at fixed heights. No,
think from the floor upward.
Consider: ferns. The walls inside
inform the walls outside. As if
an alkaline substance coats
their sensors. Consider: oneself.
Ask generations, the emotionality
in cells. My back is to the valley
because I need to be taken
by surprise, might be the only
way to be reached, the alabaster
core of my spiral. The indoor
window faces another indoor
window. I must find the pressure
points because the hair of
a monster sometimes appears
on the back of my coat.

ii.

That the depth of longing is measurable,
so I dig, try to leave it there
to enrich the soil. Amaranth will grow
as it has for centuries. On the way down
the hill I trip on a tree and face up
into the sky I fall, stare gone in the face,
recall the teacher who didn't know
what to say about light the color
of margarine. The light seemed
to pulse from the façade of the brick
building, so instead of saying
that he had nothing to say he said
nothing at all, and we turned into notes.

iii.

The wind made the light and an ash
tree seem one, animated yet mortal,
and then it ceased. For a moment
I thought the statue in the park
was me, not *of me*. (Sometimes one
needs to tell someone to go away.)
He was an admiral—some name
I hadn't heard. The winterberries
from afar look like specks of blood
on the snow, like perforation,
but I digress. As a child I related
more to adults, remember
misinterpreting situations
or at least this is what I was told.

iv.

But I am here. The condensation
on the inside frozen to the window
—the pattern an electrocardiogram
overlooking a more abstract
landscape. I went too far inside
while outside. The river is almost
fully frozen over. I remember
the last time, years ago, a red fox
crossed the river that early morning.
But here, the threat of slippery
snow almost covering the once
bare earth. It's suffocating audible
to trees. But the contrast of the more
impressive cliff face and snow,
and I recall the benign face
of the boy writing his name
with a tree branch in cement.

V.

vi.

There must be other survivors.
I hadn't acknowledged
the language of ferns. What's
the price of hope anyway? Have I
accepted the apology to myself?
This river, by not answering,
addressed my questions. There
will be a last note and it will sing.
Years ago I fell into
the gap between Z and A.

vii.

My imagination keeps me away
from night. The slant of it.
The milky light doesn't consider
these notes the feeling of a cello
swelling in a bathtub. Instead,
I try to eat all of the fallen snow
outside. Arctic air stings
the face and my throat sore
from the salt. My nose bled
out into the snow—a succession
of *I belong here* notes
as I stare into a tablespoon
reclining in the snow. Otherwise,
I'm whole and there's logic
to memory, until there isn't—
I live inside a cello. The surgery
changed my face. I believe
the strings protect me. My body
continued without its head.
The head said, *fortitude has limits,*
so our standards need to change. This
is to say those strangling tumors, that
my body is a bundle of nerves, that
I no longer recognize my voice.

viii.

I'm an idle cement truck
as succinct as cinnamon. Perhaps
this explains the euphoria
and desire the length of
the alphabet. My doctor
reminds me that semen
is not a synonym for sperm.

ix.

This intimate street. A used cello,
preposterous in a storefront window.
A utility man climbing down a manhole.
But beforehand when I looked
at his calloused hands, he dropped
a small cardboard box into the snow.
His hands looked even larger. Desire
whispered, *thieving can also be wanting
what someone is willing to give or have taken
from them.* But the private unspeakable
things taken from me burrowed
themselves somewhere outside my reach
—their walls curve like ribs of a whaling
boat, a boat poxed with barnacles.

x.

The snow-in-the-face walk
brought me to a white rabbit
who's all-eyes and safe,
for now. Also, the sheet of paper
with a boot print and the
disfigured snowman. Charcoal
because of contrast—this
lasting expression of concern
on your face. I am lesser from
wanting, yet when you I
I am more. My experience is that
indoor snow will come, tenuous
for the obvious reasons, once
I've taken in the stiff bed sheets—
yes, the sky's a place for fucking.
I found a silver-colored condom
wrapper. Yes, I slept with the snowman.
In other words, I want to bed
the monster who withheld the password.
The elements of impulse subtle
and everywhere—ask any lover.

xi

How much does sorrow influence
harmony anyway? The long version
doesn't need to be told. A teacher
told me to not write poems
about the heart or to end them
with similes. The man inside
listening to the man outside
said, *testosterone gets a bad rap*,
—without it one would expand
and crash. I will need to rub
the controlled substance
on my shoulders. But back to
the surgical theater which could
be an office without windows.
The operating table, or was it a bed,
held me during the impromptu
echocardiogram. They recorded
all the ways. I kept the echo
at heart's length, noticed all
the instruments that would be used
later to not only open, then
the fluorescent lights closed in on me.

xii

I am not a statue. Not a cello.
Not a poem. There's the danger of feeling
more, un-tethered, but the opposite's also
true. When I try to say something complicated
and don't know where the language is headed
I look up and to the left. Is this faith?
When I speak now I discern a new frequency
and different others listen. It snowed
a few inches overnight, yet the irradiating sun.
Did my lizard brain intuit or detect the cancer
when, as a breached baby, I first saw light?

xiii

I'm distracted by my body.
~~After surgery and beside~~
~~my awareness of nothingness~~
~~a mass, a mass that would later~~
~~be identified as a blood clot~~
~~imposing as a testicle.~~
My body is distracted by me.
I'm discouraged by my body.
~~After surgery my penis~~
~~swelled to the shape and size~~
~~of a large yam, the local~~
~~anesthetic got trapped there.~~
My body is by me discouraged.
~~The gait of my almost bow-~~
~~legged walk and the gait~~
~~of my unfamiliar telling voice.~~

xiv.

~~And the one testicle that remained, and worked, became slightly left of center and~~ my right leg became slightly longer than the left, and I stumbled outside. And then 17 years later, like negative capability, like a cicada, like insight, ~~the other extraction. And then I stumbled inside~~ which means that I had options. ~~That the *in* in loneliness was ensnared by *extraction*. That I will stutter~~ over other words too.

xv.

Outside: a plane at dawn
stitches the sky and the flickering
red light from a tower. Outside:
a police officer directs traffic
around the tow truck
locking itself like a tumor
to a car. Outside: snow,
like flattened cotton balls,
drifts and collects onto
pavement. Inside: the red
amaryllis stands, a siren
mounted to a pole top, and
the teakettle's pre-whistle
escalation. I move it
to an unlit burner. Inside:
I crack an egg on the side
of the skillet the size of
one cracked egg, ~~think
that without testes no one
in my image~~ and say aloud
"I never wanted children
anyway." Inside: the air purifier's
flashing red light, so I change
the carbon filter, then
reset it. ~~Inside: I remember
my first wet dream~~ Inside:

I'm indecisive about taking
a shower, re-learning
my body. Inside: I'm aware
now of my own heartbeat.

xvi.

Inside: the radiologist said, *you're going to live.*
Inside: looking out to a couple who kiss,
then walk in opposite directions. ~~Outside:
the man with shoulder blades the shape of
a night cloud said to me, *we are friends.*
as far as I'm concerned.~~ Inside: I decide
I don't believe him. Inside: looking out
to the swirling snow the color of margarine.

AFTERWORD

The second testicular cancer diagnosis came seventeen years after the first orchiectomy. One year earlier, the oncologist told me that I no longer needed to see him because the chances of a second occurrence were, *one in a million.*

I started writing the "Winterberries" poems just a few weeks prior to this second diagnosis. It was as if the body, my body, was communicating the diagnosis, writing the poem for me, but the mind, my mind, wasn't listening/converting/translating this information. I continued to revise these poems and write new ones while I waited in doctors' offices and at home waiting for the eventual procedure. All of the sections were written while I listened to Bach's *Die Kunst der Fuge* which remained unfinished due to his death.

The surgical team detected a heart irregularity while I was conscious on the operating table. Once the electrocardiogram machine was rolled over from another building and the electrodes affixed to my chest and connected to this machine they diagnosed me, *atrial fibrillation, and we can proceed with the extraction.*

ACKNOWLEDGMENTS
(and sometimes appearing in earlier versions)

JOURNALS

Action, Spectacle: "Bloodroot" + "Swamp Rose" // *The Arkansas International:* "Sheep Laurel" // *Barnstorm Journal*: "Always Something Falling" // *Barrow Street*: "Winterberries IV" + "Winterberries VI" + "Winterberries XIV" // *Bombay Gin*: "Winterberries XIII" + "Winterberries XVI" // *Chautauqua:* "Ecosystem" // *Hoxie Gorge*: "Winterberries VII" + "Winterberries XI" // *Louisville Review*: "James Schuyler to John Ashbery" + "Blue" // *The McNeese Review*: "Regarding What Was Lost Before I Knew It Was Taken" // *Meridian*: "A Housefly" // *Nashville Review*: "Comeuppance" // *Negative Capability Press:* "The Estate" // *Oversound:* "The Crumpled Paper" // *Pangyrus:* "On Variation" // *Paperbark*: "Viridescent Varieties" + "A Definition of Loss" + "Interrupted Fern" // *Poetry Northwest:* "On the Other Side" // *Potomac Review:* "Iron" // *Ruminate*: "Winterberries II" // *Sixth Finch*: "Winterberries IX" + "Winterberries X" // *Sonora Review*: "The Corridor" // *South Dakota Review*: "The Blue Vehicle" // *Tammy:* "Clouds" // *Thrush Poetry Journal*: "Floriculture" // *Typo*: "Ashbery" + "Too Bright for Landscapes" // *Water-Stone Review*: "The Geranium" // *Wilderness House Literary Review*: "Dear James Schuyler,"

ANTHOLOGIES

"Colored Condoms" appears in *From the Belly: Poets Respond to Gertrude Stein's Tender Buttons (Vol 1)*. (The Word Works)

"Limbs" appears in *From the Belly: Poets Respond to Gertrude Stein's Tender Buttons (Vol 2)*. (The Word Works)

"Narrative" appears in *The Experiment Will Not Be Bound: An Experimental Anthology of American Writing:* (Unbound Editions)

"Winterberries I" + "Winterberries XV" appear in *In the Tempered Dark* (Black Lawrence Press)

ARCHIVE

"It Fell"—the video and poem itself will be in the Poetic Phonotheque archive: www.poeticphonotheque.com

FILM

"It Fell" appeared in the 2024 International Festival of Winter Cinema in amiskwaciwâskahikan (Edmonton, Canada), in the legendary snow theatre on February 9th, 2024, in programming partnership with Silver Skate, at Wilfrid Laurier Park. "It Fell" also appeared in REELpoetry 2024.

THANK YOU

I must provide heartfelt thanks to Alexandria Peary for selecting this book for the 2024 Granite State Poetry Contest and for her thoughtful introduction; to Nossrat Yassini and the Yassini family for their generous support; to UNH's Jaed Coffin and James Krasner for developing the prize and Danielle Jones and Mal Dinaro for their continued commitment to administering the prize in all the ways that that is possible; to Ashley Halsey and Molly McGrath at Pink Eraser Press for their beautiful editing, design, and assembly; to Dan Beachy-Quick and Lisa Lewis for their thoughtful blurbs; and to this too abbreviated list of folks who have supported me and my work over the years: Aimee Harrison, Amaranth Borsuk, Anna Ross, Antonio Ochoa, Betsy Sholl, Brad Richard, Carrie Bennett, Charles Kell, Cheryl Clark Vermeulen, Claudia Keelan, Cole Swensen, Craig Morgan Teicher, Danielle Beazer Dubrasky, David Wojahn, Derek Pollard, Donald Revell, Ed Madden, Gabrielle Calvocoressi, Jack Myers, Jennifer Martelli, JenMarie Macdonald, Jessica Bozek, Jody Gladding, Jonathan Weinert, Judi Silverman, Karren Alenier, Kate Faragher Houghton, Lisa Lewis, Liz Young, Mark Cox, Megan Alpert, Michael Walsh, Nancy White, Nano Taggart, Natalie Young, Nida Sinnokrot, Oliver Strand, Patrick Davis, Peter Campion, Peter Covino, Ralph Pennel, Rob MacDonald, Ron Mohring, Ron Spalletta, Rosann Kozlowski, Stephen Tapscott, Sue Standing, Talvikki Ansel, Tanya Whiton, Timothy Liu, Willa Carroll, Wyn Cooper; to all of my students who taught me, and so many others.

The Nossrat Yassini Poetry Festival at UNH celebrates the power of poetry to unify, bring people together, and build a better community. Poetry is the oldest literary art form and the one we turn to in times of great joy, sorrow, and inspiration. Because we treasure and remember the poems that have influenced our lives, celebrating poetry can bring us together in uniquely powerful ways. This world class festival brings together poets, students, teachers, and poetry lovers of all kinds to experience the poetic richness of New Hampshire and the New England community.

Yas Press, housed in the University of New Hampshire's English Department, publishes three books a year featuring the best poetry in New Hampshire: an anthology of teen poetry, an anthology of USNH student poetry, and a previously unpublished poetry collection of extraordinary quality written by an emerging or established New Hampshire poet. These prize-winning publications are made possible through the generous support of the YAS Foundation in honor of poet and poetry lover, Nossrat Yassini. In addition, The Nossrat Yassini Poetry Prize—an annual award given each year to a first book published by a U.S. poet of extraordinary promise—is managed by the Press.

www.ingramcontent.com/pod-product-compliance
Lightning Source LLC
Chambersburg PA
CBHW060613080526
44585CB00013B/802